MW00977261

HERE I GO, TORCHING

HERE I GO, TORCHING

Poems by Carlina Duan

Winner of the 2015
Edna Meudt Memorial Award

National Federation of State Poetry Societies, Inc.
www.nfsps.com

Here I Go, Torching
© 2015 by Carlina Duan

All rights reserved. No part of this work may be reproduced or transmitted in any form or by any means, electronic or mechanical, or by use of any information storage or retrieval system, except as may be expressly permitted by the author.

Published May 2015
The National Federation of State Poetry Societies, Inc.
www.nfsps.com

Editing and design by Kathy Lohrum Cotton
Cover illustration, *Moon Girls*, by Grace Ludmer
Author photograph by Meghal Janardan

Printed in the United States of America
CreateSpace, Charleston, South Carolina

ISBN-13: 978-1511807005
ISBN-10: 1511807008

for my parents,

for Karen—

ài, and love, and love again.

CONTENTS

FOREWORD

Carlina Duan was a University of Michigan senior when she submitted a manuscript to the National Federation of State Poetry Societies' first online contest. NFSPS began to receive and process applications and manuscripts through online manager Submittable. com for the 2015 College/University-Level Poetry Competition.

After months of honing contest mechanics, the three-member committee, plus our first online-manuscript judges—James F. Ahearn, Jim Barton and Rosemerry Wahtola Trommer—announced two fine young poets as winners. For her manuscript, *Here I Go, Torching*, Carlina Duan of Ann Arbor, Michigan, was named winner of the Edna Meudt Memorial Award, which includes this chapbook.

In her application, Duan wrote, "I am curious how my responsibility as a poet intersects with my responsibility toward social change. How can I use my poetry as spark for movement? As an aspiring teacher of poetry, I'm interested in understanding how poems can operate as effective methods of social change, and how poems can encourage us to open windows, flip the familiar back into the funky, the urgent, the new."

We hope you will experience her "spark for movement" as Duan challenges prejudice and encourages us to "open windows."

Chairman Shirley Blackwell, New Mexico
Chapbook Editor Kathy Cotton, Illinois
Committee Member Heather Holland, Utah

FROM THE JUDGES

Here I Go, Torching by Carlina Duan was selected from manuscripts submitted by students from across the United States to the 2015 NFSPS College/University-Level Poetry Competition. Each of three independent judges made his or her choices for the top six manuscripts, assigning each a score from 1 to 10. Duan received the highest score for the Meudt contest. Following are excerpts from the judges' comments.

JAMES AHEARN, MICHIGAN

Here I Go, Torching is a manuscript with extraordinary disparate imagery, sometimes seemingly unrelated, such as snow and muscle or turnips and joy, that somehow finds a way to fit together. Situational turn-about also intrigued me, as in the final two lines of the last poem where I found "…cotton napkins: waiting for you to unfold." Such nuggets among these poems are golden experiences.

JIM BARTON, ARKANSAS

Fresh, invigorating language and imagery; outstanding grasp of poetics. Knows just exactly when to end each poem for maximum effect. A joy to read and reread!

ROSEMERRY WAHTOLA TROMMER, COLORADO

Fabulous. This collection of poems explores so many layers of identity—relationships with culture, with family, with lovers, with self. The language is fresh and surprising, and the simple syntax works well for conveying complex ideas. Every poem struggles, and is beautiful in its struggle. A courageous collection.

ACKNOWLEDGMENTS

Endless praise above my head for all of the gracious brains and breaths who have made these poems possible. I continue to feel empowered by so many wondrous teachers, family, and friends who have lifted me up with their wisdom and love.

Endless gratitude for Jeremy Chamberlin, Nate Marshall, Jeff Kass, Keith Taylor, Anne Curzan, and Cody Walker for their mentorship, teaching, deep kindnesses, and unwavering belief in my work—and in me. You all inspire me to greater heights.

Thank you to my brainy and beautiful friends: I am filled with light for knowing and growing with all of you. Gratitude for my "Michigan in Color" co-editors and sisters: Teresa Mathew, Ryan Moody, and Nour Soubani, for their courage and devotion to storytelling in and by communities of color. A huge shout out to The Neutral Zone, VOLUME Youth Poetry Project, and Red Beard Press: best space(s) in the nation, home and heart; you taught me first.

I am indebted to the National Federation of State Poetry Societies for their generosity and warmth, and humbled by their support for emerging writers. Thank you especially to Kathy Cotton, Shirley Blackwell and Heather Holland for helping make this chapbook possible.

Lastly, I am deeply thankful for my family—for raising me, lifting me, and nourishing me with their languages, stories, and love. Thank you to my sister, Karen Duan—graceful, patient, wise, my lifelong superheroine. Thank you to my parents, Cunming Duan and Min Zhang, who own excellent hearts. Their sacrifices, empathy, and daily teachings have humbled me as a poet and as a human being. I have been—and will continue to be—sustained by such power, and such love.

–Carlina

PLEDGE OF ALLEGIANCE

my mother is not from your country
filled with chocolates and rain.
don't ask me where my solitude comes from—
in this country I know we floss our teeth.
in this country I know how to swim, how to
part my lips. what's black, & what's bent.
what's not mine to touch.

salt sparkles on sidewalks of blank snow,
in this country my lungs are strong.
my elbows: sharp, I get that from my mother.

we do not pour soy sauce on our rice.
we do not eat our cheeseburgers
with quiet hands, we toast white
breads and smash their faces thick
with butter.

my mother is not from your country, and I am
her daughter. don't ask me what it's like
being small and Chinese.
I have tupperware and eat almonds—
I have pride: warm and plump, like a moon.

my mother does not own a laundromat, or
a takeout restaurant, she waters orchids
and doesn't look your president in the eye.

my mother is not from your country,

and I am not ashamed.

I slip my hands through her wise hair,

& blacken,
& blacken—

& keep.

GAME BOY ADVANCE

hover in the dumbstruck night.
milk in lonely cups, video games,
sister's pink forehead shining
in the dark. her spit, starred.
too embarrassed to ask boss
for a lunch break, she eats
homemade edamame
at a Starbucks, four
hours after her shift—
Don't tell mom.
napkins, blood
orange juicing her
hands. mouth round,
a leash. what she'll
do for minimum
wage. small animals
flashing across her
screen. night in our jaws,
in our teeth, until I grind.
moon flashing
like a white rumor
until I snap, call her
a child; swerve and yell
in her bed. *I don't*
like to see you working
so hard, I push against
her elbow, our cheeks
touch. she says
nothing. presses
the A button. kills
an animal mercilessly
with her thumb.

WHAT YOU LOOKIN' AT, CHINK

she yelled out the car window. I clutched
the soft drink in my yellow hand,
turned paw at the intersection. bodies
brushed past me. the straw stuck
ghostly to my snout. the light flashed red
then green. she squeezed past the biker
lane. I took a sip and the cold shot down
a throat, wetted my whiskers. inside
a furry ear, the word CHINK swerved
and thrashed.

the Chink is a mammal who loves dirt
and kernels of white rice. the Chink
is a mammal who sharpens pencils,
twitches beneath a blank sky.
the Chink flashes her a look like a switch-
blade, eats muffins, drives at precise
speed limits, the Chink clenches
and unclenches a mouth.

beware of the Chink: how it bites.

SEVERED

after you left the country, there was an oil spill
off the Louisiana coast. birds coiled their wings.
fish strummed through the water, then died.

in the kitchen, I placed pickles on squares of
whole grain bread. outside, puddles
stretched in rainbow grease.

somewhere, you pushed a hand into the
cash register. swallowed a melatonin pill, sucked
in scents of gasoline, grass. in another continent,

you flashed your knees. off the coastline,
a wing puckered black. we were too far away
to notice. I wished, many times, for your hand.

after you left the country, a small field of silence.
artichokes locked inside a can. dead amphibians
and my small chest, ghosting and fuming

after you. meanwhile, ache smoothed its fingers
on the nape of my neck. told me to keep quiet, tread
water. forget the leathery strap of your name.

PACKING LUNCH ON ANN STREET

red and purple candies spill into a plastic bag.
cherry, grape: traipse liquid in my mouth.
through cavities: I sleep. sugar stays.
on Ann Street, I pluck tight strings and forget
the hot slash of your name. my mother salts

a hard-boiled egg. my sister catches salt-
water on a toothbrush from the sink. bagged
celery stalks. black nose hairs. I forget
how grief chases the pink mouth,
tussles the teeth. begs to stay.

in the neighborhood, recyclables stay
in green bins. fathers stay, too: cast cubes of salt
onto driveways. we are flush with snow. mouths
of dogs flip open. our pink tongues hang. I bag
grief between two slices of white bread. I forget

with every bite. you-died you-died. forget-
ful, hoarse, I try calling you back. grief brays. I stay
inside the house with yellow lights. I eat a bag
full of candies with my fist. once, salt
slid across your tongue and you mouthed

the words to a Joni Mitchell song: *a mouth
like yours*, I had a mouth. it was yours. I forget
all the noisy ways you were mine, scattered like salt
across a table. my mouth sticks. grief stays.
outside, birds swallow, you crumble. I shut the bag.

WHAT I'VE LOST

teeth. metallic parts of head-
phones, bad machinery. sticks
of lead. loves I once pressed
my lips to, firm and hard, on
their whole, precious throats.
entire countries with darts of
black pepper streaked across
the napkins, entire countries
bleating with the creamy milk
of goats. it is absolute: this loss.
rivers and eyelashes. onions
waggling their roots. what I
will never know: new sisters
and stones curled into the center
of a palm. what I've missed: kernels
of corn, kettles of water.

I am lonely, in my lonely chest.

birds traipse out windows. flags
lift their red and floppy throats.
cars shout, I will never hear them.
I want to catch so much of this earth
on the gentle tongue, but
outside: there is only snow.
and inside: there is only muscle.
only what I can give and flex—
which is to say, inside: there is
a moon in me, a heart

that swamps and swamps.
today: oil and vessel. turnips
I fried for dinner. joy I got
from touching a friend's humble
face. the monthly blood. the honest
stutter. what I place my paws on:
only rain, only squares of papaya,
and the hundred lives in me all
hard and tender, eager to sprout.

I WASN'T JOKING

I got a collarbone. I got
an untidy mouth. I got
a scalp where rain darts,
watch my palms chase
through the head's black
gully—in each arm-
pit I grow and grow
the flossy hairs. in each
armpit I sweat, sprout.
I got a yodel in me, watch
me flex precise. watch
the pinkest muscle: won't
give up my tongue for no
one—how it slices
and drums. in a dream
men told me I was small
and what did I know,
woman with modest toes
and knees. when they
patted me on the head I
slashed the dirt, I slashed
the gladiola, nipples flowered
like purple planets, all my
hair chirped, I opened
my mouth and let my
hundred-teeth show:
saliva, gum. canines
glinted, flashed

the flash of rivers.
when I bit my bottom
lip they said

Oh

and I turned
vicious: girl
stroking the earth
with two biceps, let
no one take my
tongue. I got a yodel
in me, won't back down
without parting my lips
wet and eager
for the flight—

HERE I GO, TORCHING

he came over. asked, *what are you?*
I said it out loud. he said, *oh,*
disappointed. *I thought you*
were Malaysian. I turned small
and wiped my ash-mouth. his
tasted like green onions, lampshades.
light gone bad. he said, *konichiwa,*
then kissed me till I twanged. till
the muscle in my face snapped.
freckles all over his arm: small
brown rhymes. my body:
bilingual threat. muscle
in my tongue, in each slice
I speak. black plain of hair.
plain of mouth, of meat. he
pushed up my shirt, ricochet.
gunpowder teeth, he wanted neither
of my tongues. just gold hoops
in my ears. metal in the tank,
in the bed. I'm Chinese, see me
and my pulled muscle. see him
and his snapped trigger. our sputter
and splash into the night. glow of my
own simple skin. quietly, he stayed.

I didn't speak.

SHUT DOWN

the night I decided to leave you,
the government shut down.

my knees were cold.
I drank tap water and listened to jazz.

somewhere: 80,000 federal workers
furloughed. a million asked to work

without pay. I poured olive oil
into a pan, my black hair crackled blacker.

on television: the president
& his moist lip.

outside, a truck flared its wheels.
I undressed, and watched my bare stomach

bloat beneath a light-
bulb. quietly, & curried with rage,

I sliced
a plum.

ON A BAD DAY

after Mary Oliver, "Wild Geese"

you do not have to be good.
you do not have to rinse your hands
beneath the sink, after slicing the sharp
brick of cheddar, wringing & waiting out
the salt to come. you do not have to say
his name. or call it back,
the way a planet does, the way geese do
solemnly in the cold. you do not have to
pound your fists into the plastic bags,
searching for a gallon of milk,
a sealed can of sugar. you do not have to
wrest open, or harm.

you only have to let your ache
harvest the ordinary walls, your
ordinary knees. you only have to honor
the hot, hot rain. give me your
turbulence, and I'll hand it back—
remember your red blood, his
big hands, shameful circles
of deli sandwich meat in
the dining hall,

you do not have to wait for him.
you only have to go, & go.

meanwhile, the bakery
glazes its donuts.

meanwhile, your father
drives to work. meanwhile,
your mother places sheaves
of dried apricots into a jar,
waiting for you to come home,
& you knit your eyebrows
& check the tables for mold—
wherever you are, no matter
how lonely, praise your
simple chest. the silverware,
the cotton napkins: waiting
for you to unfold.

CARLINA DUAN

Photo by Meghal Janardan

Carlina Duan is a poet and journalist from Ann Arbor, Michigan. A 2015 graduate of the University of Michigan with a BA in English and creative writing, Duan has won multiple Hopwood awards and writing prizes, worked as an editor for *The Michigan Daily*, and spent many sunrises on her purple bike. She is one of the founding editors of Ann Arbor's Red Beard Press, a youth-driven publishing company, and also the co-author of the poetry collection *Electric Bite Women* (2013) with poet Haley Patail. As a U.S. Fulbright scholar, Duan will teach English in Malaysia.

Her poetry collection, *Here I Go, Torching*, encompasses everyday narratives of loves, losses and ailments, documenting "American girlhood" and ultimately redefining it. In these poems, Duan questions: What, and who, is an "American girl"? Who is allowed access to "American girlhood"? What happens when the girl comes from a bilingual family of Chinese immigrants, living in the Midwest? These poems include narratives of new feminism, heritage, rage, joy—culminating in a series that reflects coming of age in the 21st century as a Chinese-American girl, sister, daughter, citizen.

THE JUDGES

JAMES F. AHEARN, a perennial prizewinner at the NFSPS Annual Poetry Contest awards, has consistently placed in the top ten in multiple categories for more than a decade. His poems have appeared regularly in *Encore* and anthologies published by the Poetry Society of Michigan (PSM). Ahearn coauthored with Joye Giroux *A Reintroduction to Poetry: A Poet's Workshop Experiences and Tips* (2009) and also published essays and poetry in *Boundary Waters Journal*. He has served PSM as vice president for four years, president from 2010 to 2013, and annual contest coordinator since 2009. He lives in Rochester, Michigan, where he conducts a monthly poetry group.

JIM BARTON serves as first vice president and membership chair for NFSPS and treasurer of both the Poets' Roundtable of Arkansas and his local branch. He has four collections of poetry, including the Morris Chapbook Award winner, *At the Bird Museum*. He has won awards nationwide and his poetry appears in such venues as *The Lyric, The Mid-America Poetry Review, Louisiana Literature* and the *Mississippi Review*. He is a convention and seminar speaker throughout the South and a national and regional poetry judge. Barton believes that a world without poetry is a world without light and that the future of poetry is bright indeed.

ROSEMERRY WAHTOLA TROMMER lives in southwest Colorado. Her poetry has appeared in *O Magazine*, on *A Prairie Home Companion*, in back alleys, and on river rocks. Her poetry collections include *The Less I Hold, The Miracle Already Happening: Everyday Life with Rumi, Intimate Landscape* and *Holding Three Things at Once* (Colorado Book Award finalist). She served as San Miguel County's first poet laureate and directed the Telluride Writers Guild for ten years. Trommer travels widely to perform poetry and music and to teach. Since 2004, she has maintained a poem-a-day practice. Visit her at www.wordwoman.com.

NFSPS COLLEGE/UNIVERSITY COMPETITION

A seven-member planning committee for a National Federation of State Poetry Societies college-level scholarship met on June 26, 1988, at the NFSPS convention in Salt Lake City, Utah. The committee included:

Susan Steven Chambers, Good Thunder, MN
Robert E. DeWitt, Green Cove Springs, FL
Melba C. Dungey, Morgantown, WV
Max Golightly, Provo, UT
Ralph Hammond, Arab, AL
Edna Meudt, Dodgeville, WI
Golda Foster Walker, Baton Rouge, LA

The scholarship was subsequently named in loving memory of Edna Meudt, who died in April 1989. Meudt was a charter member and past president of NFSPS and a member of the Wisconsin Fellowship of Poets. Her wisdom and staunch support helped to make the dream of this award a reality.

In 1999, Florence Kahn, a long-time member of the Miami-Earth Chapter of the Florida State Poets Association, made a generous bequest to the NFSPS scholarship fund. At the 1999 convention in Atlanta, Georgia, the name of the award was changed to the NFSPS Scholarship Award, with one manuscript chosen for the Edna Meudt Memorial Award and one for the Florence Kahn Memorial Award.

At the 2001 convention in Melbourne, Florida, the name of the award was changed to the NFSPS College/University-Level Poetry Competition. It was open to juniors and seniors at accredited colleges and universities. At the 2003 convention in Sioux Falls, South Dakota, the competition was opened to freshmen and sophomores as well.

For the 2015 competition, manuscripts were accepted and judged online for the first time, utilizing the submissions manager, Submittable.com. Also a first for the 2015 contest was the publication and marketing of the chapbooks as perfect-bound paperbacks. The committee included Shirley Blackwell of New Mexico, Kathy Cotton of Illinois, and Heather Holland of Utah.

Annual contest guidelines are posted on the NFSPS website, www.nfsps.com.

43520446R00023

Made in the USA
Middletown, DE
11 May 2017